Hey Dad,

What Did You Do

During the Cold War?

Memoirs from someone who worked
for the Pentagon 30 years in
Operations Research and Intelligence

Robert E. Schmaltz

Printed in the United States of America

ISBN: 978-0-578-02694-7

Dedication

To

Lorraine
my wife and love of my life

Robert, Thomas, Steven
our three sons of whom we are so proud

Jason, Gretchen, Ben, Charlotte, Kathryn
our very special grandchildren

Contents

List of Photographs

Foreword

I grew up in Scranton, PA. The schools were good and those were good years. We were relatively poor, but we didn't know it. How my parents raised four kids during the 1910s, 20s, and 30s seems like an impossible task to me today.

After I graduated from high school, I went to Lehigh University. At that time in 1944 there were few men around. When you reached 18 years of age, you were immediately drafted. In November when I was 18, I appeared before the draft board to ask for a two-month deferment to finish my semester at school. I did get the extension and in the meantime enlisted in the Air Force as an Aviation Cadet.

When I tell people now, especially military people, that I worked for the Pentagon for 30 years they give me a strange look as though something was wrong with me. Actually, a lot of the experiences were interesting and exciting. However, some were not.

The Cold War lasted from 1949 (arguable 1948 for some) to 1991. 1949 was a special year for me since I started my first job working for the government as a civilian for the Pentagon. And most importantly, it was the year I got married, a marriage that lasted for 59 years.

My areas of work involved Intelligence 1949 - 1966, Systems Analysis/Operations Research 1966 – 1978 and consulting part-time on Information Systems 1978 – 1998. Hence, my working career coincided with the Cold War. Also, I was in the Army Air Force for two years during World War II (a navigator) and in the Air Force Reserves for 25 years with assignments to HQ US Air Force and HQ Strategic Air Command.

I have a BS degree in Industrial Engineering, an MSBA (Operations Research) from George Washington University and taught part-time for two years at American University.

My experiences discussed in this book are in the context of the Cold War. The book can be categorized in the following areas biography, history and military.

1

The Beginning of My Journey

A girl in her 20s was filling out a form and asked me if I knew the date. I told her it was the 7th of December. I asked her if she knew what December 7th signified. She thought a minute and asked if it was someone's birthday. I said no, it is Pearl Harbor Day. She responded "Oh yes, I saw that movie and thought Ben Affleck was a great actor."

I was surprised. However, this is just another example of the younger generation's lack of knowledge about history. If they don't know what Pearl Harbor Day is, how can they possibly know what the 40-year Cold War was? You cannot blame our young people for not knowing some history since it is not taught in our school systems.

I had three reasons to write this book. The first one is to try to inform some people about the nature and significance of the Cold War. I am concerned about the lack of understanding of our history, including the Cold War, since people won't understand what could happen in the future. The public is not informed about the feelings and fear during different dangerous events during the Cold War, such as the Kruschev – Kennedy stand off on the Soviet Missile Blockade of Cuba, the Berlin Blockade, the first Soviet manned cosmonaut in orbit, Soviet ICBM testing, etc. It was a stressful and dangerous time. Today, there are few young Americans aware of that situation. I can still remember the feelings of many people - the uncertainty, worry, fear and anxiety over many of the Cold War events. The people were afraid that a nuclear war would affect everyone in the US. There was a rush to build bomb shelters – my daughter-in-law recalls that when she was in grade school they had a drill to get under their desks in case of an attack.

The second reason is to inform my three sons and five grandchildren about the Cold War and my experiences during this period and better understand me as an imperfect father. Some of the experiences could not be discussed when they were young,

And a third reason was to identify the contribution made by some of the military personnel, especially those in the Air Force Strategic Air Command. I noted that many of them were hard working and had a stressful life. I don't believe people know of this sacrifice and the impact it had on their families.

These were some of the thoughts that inspired me to write this book. The book discusses my experience only in parts of the Cold War. My major point is that the Cold War was a big deal in our country's history. I hope that this book conveys some of these thoughts.

The book started out as a description of my work experience over 50 years. However, as I did the research I became aware of the significance of the war, the role of Target Intelligence, Strategic Air Command capabilities, the Space Race and technological competition. This resulted in a story of my work experience within the context of the Cold War.

Although I worked for the Pentagon (i.e., the Air Force and the Department of Defense, Defense Intelligence Agency) at times my work required me to be physically located in: a building called "The Brewery" in the Pentagon parking lot; a high rise building in Rosslyn, VA; and the Library of Congress. I also traveled to installations in Germany, Japan, Hawaii, Alaska, the CIA, the NSA, the ACIC, and the Army Arlington Hall. I enjoyed my work and was never bored.

Since this book is about my work experience, I have presented some background of the situation and organization at the beginning, followed by my work experience in the organization. This procedure and the description of the Cold War present the context in which my experiences took place.

The Pentagon

2

Pre Cold War

Enlisting Problem

On March 11, 1944 I enlisted as an Aviation Cadet in the Army Air Force. Well, it wasn't that simple. First, I had to pass a physical and mental test. The mental test was no problem, but the physical was. A young Second Lieutenant called me into his office and said, "Son, do you want to fly?"

I replied “Yes Sir.”

“Then gain 20 pounds and come back in two weeks.”

I weighed 128 pounds. I was in college at the time and asked my doctor to help me. He said there is no way you can gain 20 pounds in two weeks, but come back in two weeks and I will tell you what to do. I went back the day before I was due to report again and he told me to get a bunch of bananas and when I get up the next day for my physical, eat the bananas and drink lots of water, which would turn into lead. I ate the bananas, drank the water, got on the scale and got in the Air Force.

Going home on a trolley between Allentown and Bethlehem, PA I nearly exploded.

Basic Training

When I received my orders to report, my father walked with me to the train station. When he waved goodbye, that was the first time I saw him cry. I took the train from Scranton PA to the Army Induction Center near Harrisburg. The first thing we did was get rid of our civilian clothes and get Army clothes, including heavy overcoats. Then, a week later we took a train to Biloxi MS. This was one of many train rides I took during my time in the service. All the trains had stiff straw weaved backs – no reclining lounge seats. At times, we actually slept on the floor. We were young then.

The basic training was 10 weeks with no weekend time off. We were all out of shape for the training. We had to take a physical exam that included a series of shots e.g., small pox, typhoid, tetanus, etc. I was one of those people who fainted whenever they stuck me with a needle.

We also took some classification tests. Later I was told that I was going into the Artillery. I immediately had them check my records because I was classified as a draftee and not as an Aviation Cadet. When they checked again I did have a draftee and Cadet serial number. Luckily, I kept the Cadet number to go into the Air Force. I think what happened was that I enlisted in the Aviation Cadet Program and at a later date my draft board drafted me.

The training included close order drills and one hour of physical training when we woke up. I wasn't used to this schedule. They showed us movies about Germany and Japan as well as Army regulations. Another movie was on venereal diseases – syphilis, gonorrhea, etc. with related model examples. The movie also covered condoms and a Pro-Kit to use after sex.

I took Basic Training at Keesler Air Field, in Biloxi, Mississippi. At the time, Biloxi was the shrimp capital of the US and today it is a gambling casino area. Neil Simon, the famous playwright took Basic Training at Biloxi about the same time; he wrote a book and a successful Broadway play "Biloxi Blues" about his experience. It was fairly accurate except for the crazy drill instructor. The training was uneventful except for the discipline, drilling, firing of guns and drinking - 2.5% JAX Beer.

We took tests to determine which training school to attend to become a pilot, navigator, or bombardier. I wanted to be a navigator and was selected. I can remember when I was 17 years old I went to see the movie called "Air Force", the story of a B-17 Flying Fortress Bomber flying from the US to Hawaii on 7 December. I said to myself that I would like to be a navigator in the Air Force some day. I got my wish.

Aerial Gunnery School

Since so many aircrew members were killed in missions over Europe, all navigators and bombardiers were required to go to gunnery school. I was sent to Las Vegas Army Air Force Base to attend the B-17 Aerial Gunnery School.

After some ground classroom training we were assigned to Indian Springs Air Field outside of Las Vegas, in the desert, for Christmas week. We fired 50 caliber machine guns from all positions on a B-17 aircraft – nose, top, waist, tail and belly, against ground targets and sleeve targets towed by a B-26 aircraft. We used gun cameras against fighter planes, attacking from the open-air side gun position and the belly turret. We were so cold during this week that we wore woolen underwear and heavy overcoats at all times. There was one stove in the barracks. One impressive classroom drill was to be able to take a 50-caliber machine gun apart and put it back together in three minutes, blindfolded; this was supposed to simulate gun problems at night.

Although this was a training exercise there were many incidents that were dangerous. For example, one B-17 engine caught fire and everyone had to parachute. Since waist guns had safety cutoffs, one horizontal tail was shot off when it didn't cut off and a B-26 pilot pulling a sleeve target was very upset when the top gunner's gun was pointing at him, even though the safety on the gun was cut off.

The gambling casinos of today's Las Vegas did not exist. They were built later outside the town. One of the first casinos was run by the gangster Bugsy Seigle who opened the first one called El Rancho Vegas. We checked it out (see photo at the end of this chapter). We were not aware of Bugsy Seigle at the time. There is a movie out now called "The Marrying Man," which takes place in El Rancho Vegas.

Delays

Openings in navigation school were not always available so we were assigned to various air bases until there was an opening. This included:

- Southwest Missouri State College in Springfield. We took courses in math and science.
- La Junta Army Air Field, La Junta, Colorado. We refueled B-25 aircraft that were used to train Chinese pilots. Coming from the east, I thought Colorado was a desert, based on La Junta. There was only one bar in town with one kind of drink – Southern Comfort.
- Santa Ana Army Air Base, Santa Ana, California. I attended pre flight school ground classes and classes on how to be an officer.
- Kirtland Air Field, Albuquerque, New Mexico. We lived in a tent in the sand. I was

never sure they knew we were there because we never talked to anyone. We had to occupy ourselves by visiting the Indian ruins and the coeds at the University of New Mexico.

Navigation School

Finally, navigator school openings were available at Selman Air Field, Monroe, Louisiana. Navigation school lasted 6 months. We flew in twin-engine AT-7 planes learning dead reckoning, celestial, LORAN radar and instrument navigation. The most impressive thing to me about the training was that you could fly from Houston, Texas to Boca Raton, Florida, over water, the Gulf of Mexico, at night, by navigating only by the stars.

I graduated in July 1945 and was given orders as a navigator on B-29 aircraft at an overseas training unit in Utah. Then the atomic bomb was dropped and my orders were canceled. I was assigned to a navigators' pool at Lincoln Army Air Base, Nebraska and took some college courses at the University of Nebraska. After a while I was assigned to an administrative job at Keesler Army Air Field in Biloxi, MS. From there I went to Mitchell Air Field, New York where I was discharged. We were given the option to go to pilot training or get out, so I got out and went back to college.

When I was discharged after World War II, I returned to college, and stayed in the Air Force

Reserve for 25 years as an intelligence officer. During the Korean War, I thought I would be called up and decided that if I were, I would stay on active duty for 20 years. However, I learned later that the reason I wasn't called up as a navigator was that the names were picked in alphabetical order and by the time they reached the letter "S" they discovered that it was too much trouble to retrain the World War II Navigators instead of training new navigators.

I was very fortunate with my military experience when I was 18 - 20 years old and the fact that the atomic bomb was dropped at that time. The bomb shortened the time till the end of the war. The Japanese had 2 million ground troops waiting for our invasion and many B-29 aircraft were lost in the Pacific. If I were a year older, this story might be different.

Pre-Flight School

Pre-flight School Class at Santa Ana, California, September30, 1944. (top row, fifth from the left.)

B-17 Flying Fortress Bomber

I fired the 50-caliber machine guns in the top turret, belly turret, side opening, nose and tail guns.

50-Caliber Guns, Waist, Belly, Top

El Rancho Vegas Bar

La Junta Colorado
Army Air Field Barracks

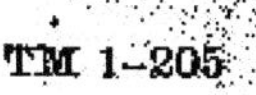

TM 1-205

TECHNICAL MANUAL No. 1-205 | WAR DEPARTMENT, WASHINGTON, *November 25, 1940.*

AIR NAVIGATION

Prepared under direction of the Chief of the Air Corps

Air Navigation Technical Manual

Aerial Gunner and Navigator Wings

Top Photo = Navigator Wings, Selman Army Air Field, Louisiana, July 1945

Bottom Photo = Aerial Gunner Wings, Las Vegas Army Air Field, Nevada, January 1945

Aviation Cadet, Officer

B-29 Super Fortress Bomber

I received orders as Navigator on a B-29 to an overseas training unit, but the atomic bomb was dropped on Japan, the war ended, and my orders were cancelled.

3

The Cold War Threats: 1949 – 1991

Significance

The Cold War was the interaction, technical competition and tensions between the Soviets and the US from 1949 to 1991. The significance of some of the events is that they could produce a trigger to set off a World War between the nuclear bombers and ICBMs of the Soviets and the nuclear bombers and ICBMs of the US. (This is discussed in more detail in Chapter 4).

Major Events

The following is a list of the significant events that could have produced a trigger, followed by a discussion of all the events of the Cold War.

Berlin Blockade 1949
Korean War 1950 – 1953
Viet Nam War 1959 – 1975
Berlin Crisis 1961
Cuban Missile Crisis 1962
Afghanistan Invasion 1979 – 1989

Highlights of All Events

1940s

The Soviets cut off all shipments to Berlin. West Berlin was declared off limits. The Berlin Blockade and related airlift were events that some considered the first true confrontation of the Cold War. It lasted 11 months. At any time during the Blockade actual fighting could occur and would have started World War III.

The Chinese Communists took over China. China became another threat.

The 40s and 50s were an intense period of social and political turmoil around the world, because of supposed foreign threats to national security.

The Soviets established the Warsaw Pact in response to NATO.

The Soviets develop the atomic bomb.

1950s

The Soviets supported the North Koreans' invasion of South Korea. (There were a few fighter aircraft flown by Soviets but it was kept quiet.) If they deployed their forces it would have become a dangerous situation. Chinese troops were involved. United Nations and US forces assisted the South Korean Army. The four years' war was one of the few instances of the Cold War that included an actual battle.

Cuban revolutionary forces took over Cuba. The Soviets supported Castro.

Soviets tested their first ICBM and launched Sputnik, the first satellite to orbit.

The US created the hydrogen bomb.

The Soviets dropped their first nuclear bomb.

There was fierce technological competition between the Soviets and the US.

The Arabs and Israel went to war in 1956.

1960s

The Soviets dropped the largest atomic bomb.

US quarantined Cuban waters in fear that the Soviets would provide the Cubans nuclear weapons in Cuba. In a standoff with the US the Soviets backed down. This was a huge event of the Cold War because we were on the brink of a nuclear war.

The Viet Nam War began; it was a critical conflict since we were concerned about the domino theory to contain communism.

US Doctrine of Massive Retaliation began.

Berlin Wall was built by Soviets to partition the city.

President Kennedy's Bay of Pigs invasion of Cuba failed.

US and Soviets were in an Arms Race – developing more nuclear weapons, nuclear weapon stockpiling, antinuclear defense systems, anti-ballistic missiles, multiple independent target re-entry vehicles, etc.

Arab – Israeli War of 1967.

1970s

Soviet troops invaded Afghanistan.

Detente Doctrine became a policy with the Soviets.

Arab – Israeli War of 1973 started when Egypt and Syria attacked Israel.

1980s

Soviets withdrew troops from Afghanistan.

Reagan rejected the Detente Doctrine while increasing military spending.

Communism continued to crumble in Eastern Europe.

Berlin Wall was dismantled.

Mikhail Gorbachev came to power in the Soviet Union.

Strategic Defense Initiative (SDI) was proposed, which would counter hostile missiles.

1990s

Summit meetings with Gorbachev diminished the Cold War

Gorbachev resigned.

USSR dissolved.

Cold War officially was over in December 1991.

This page intentionally left blank.

4
The Driving Nuclear Forces

Strategies

For a long time the US had missile superiority over the Soviets. By the beginning of the sixties, the Soviets began to catch up. On October 30, 1961 the Soviets dropped the world's largest atomic bomb. President Kennedy announced that the US would further extend nuclear weapons development, through the doctrine of Massive Retaliation. This meant that if the Soviets attacked the U.S., we would retaliate with all our nuclear bombs on B-47 and B-52 bombers, Atlas, Titan, and Minuteman Missiles. The arms race was on; neither nation wanted to prove inferior in a nuclear standoff.

Various strategies for employing nuclear weapons were discussed during the Cold War including:

- Massive Retaliation
- Counterforce Strategy – This would not really limit the damage on the US
- Finite Deterrence - This wouldn't make much difference if one system were added at a time.

The final decision was changed to a Détente Doctrine (nuclear deterrence, nuclear war avoidance). It was a relaxing or easing of tensions between the US and USSR. The other strategies were unsatisfactory; the only alternative was to maintain a strategic retaliatory force so invulnerable and so horrifying in its destructive power, no one would dare launch a first strike. Major General Glenn Kent developed some mathematical curves that showed that the other strategies were not feasible since they would destroy both countries.

Strategic Air Command (SAC)

SAC was the operational establishment in charge of land-based nuclear bomber aircraft and missiles in the strategic arsenal from 1948 to 1992. SAC became the cornerstone of US national policy.

In 1962, there were 282,723 US Air Force personnel assigned to SAC. Also, SAC built up a substantial force of jet bombers. At its peak, the SAC force included more than 1500 bombers. ICBMs became available in the late 50s. During the Cold War, SAC supported an airborne 24-hour a day EC-135 aircraft from 1961 to 1990 in Operation Looking Glass, creating an airborne command and control post in case of a nuclear attack. Also, some nuclear bombers were on a 15-minute alert, which meant that the pilot had to take off with a 15-minute notice.

General Curtis E. Lemay, the SAC commander from 1948 to 1957 stated the following in his testimony before Congress on September 23, 1956:

"...The decisive phase of the airpower battle is won or lost before the shooting war starts. This brings us again to the conclusion that the Cold War, in which the United States is now engaged, could already be part of World War III...

"Our national policy is one of deterrence... We deter by making clear that we have strength, and that its application will cost the enemy more than he could possibly gain by attacking us. Our assumption is, of course, that those who make decisions in the Soviet Bloc are not without reason – that they are not deliberately bent on suicide... They will not start a shooting war, regardless of their definition of victory, as long as it will cost them more than they can possibly gain.

"We have the strength to deter them. Today we have the ability to win the airpower battle. So today we are achieving our national aim – we are preventing a shooting war by possessing enough superiority that we are clearly ahead in the current Cold War."

Command Post Exercises (CPX)

CPXs were conducted to improve the capability of the players to respond to crises, contingencies, and general war situations by testing plans and battle staff procedures involving communication systems, issuing orders, aircraft flying to targets, ICBMs launched against targets, and bomb damage assessment conducted by the intelligence personnel.

I had a Ready Reserve Mobilization Assignment with the Intelligence Directorate, HQ Strategic Air Command for 10 years, primarily involved in Command Post Exercises (CPXs). We also visited SAC air bases and missile sites on orientation tours. A CPX was an exercise in an actual war with the Soviets in which actual aircraft flew to exercise targets and dropped simulated atomic bombs, ICBM missiles were fired, messages were exchanged (with teletype machines; there were no computers) throughout the war exercise. The Intelligence Division kept track of the war by plotting the effects of the atomic bombs dropped, the aircraft losses and the status of the war. We plotted the effects of the atomic bombs with what we called *donkey tails*, shaped like a pear to indicate the target struck and its radiation effects on a large two-story map of the Soviet Union. There were no monitors or computers like we have today. Twice a year our group in Washington, called ADVEL Group (for advanced echelon), participated in CPXs. SAC would send a plane to Washington, pick up our group and fly us to Omaha, Nebraska HQ, SAC, to augment the SAC personnel and participate in CPXs. We carried in our pockets a set of orders that stated if a real situation occurred we would be on active duty.

We were usually assigned to the 50-foot underground SAC Command Post for the CPX for the simulated war from midnight until 8 am (martinis and steak for breakfast). Initially, as stated above, the exercise atomic bombs were dropped in the Soviet Union. Once during a CPX, something strange occurred. As the exercise messages were exchanged during the war, we received a message that the cable under the Atlantic Ocean to Europe was cut. This was not an exercise message, but a real time message. We wondered whether the Soviets cut the cable during our exercise. Was this the start of the real thing, or what? Well, after a while, we found out that a fishing trawler cut the cable. We were relieved.

One humorous thing happened to our Adjutant. It was during one of our SAC tours in the underground command post where there was very little space, so they had to put the Adjutant desk in a latrine (a toilet, for you civilians). Preston was working at his desk one day when General LeMay, SAC Commander, came in and asked him what he was doing in the latrine. Preston jumped to attention in shock and said, "Sir I am putting in my time as a Reserve Officer." General LeMay left the latrine and in five minutes Preston had his own office. (You have to know who General LeMay was to appreciate this.)

When we discuss the Cold War, what major force are we talking about? We are talking about the threat of an exchange of atomic bombs from bomber aircraft and ICBMs. This does not imply that the Army and Navy didn't each make contributions in the mix of other forces. However, the Doctrine during this time period was based primarily on SAC nuclear bombers and ICBMs, e.g., Massive Retaliation, Détente, etc.

After 25 years in the Reserves and two years in World War II, I retired as a Lieutenant Colonel.

Active Duty Personnel

As a Reservist, going to various SAC bases and SAC HQ, I had the opportunity to observe the lives of active duty personnel during the Cold War. I recognized what a stressful life most of them had and the sacrifices they and their families endured. The Air Force Base at Offutt was an entirely different world than that where civilians lived off base. I'm not sure that at that time (or today) Americans were aware of their sacrifices.

Most of the military lived under stressful conditions with their work. The fact that they were the number one target for Soviet nuclear missiles made their lives that much more stressful. We saw the personnel under stress in the 50-foot underground command and control intelligence center. Obviously the families of these personnel were impacted on not only the base but also when they flew missions.

New Nuclear Mission

Over the years, the nuclear force was depleted. In 2008, nuclear organization and posture received priority attention from the Air Force. It appears that now the Air Force is going to develop a nuclear deterrence capability.

In Air Force Magazine (January 2009), Lieutenant General Robert Elder, head of the 8th Air Force, acknowledged that:

“USAF’s focus on the nuclear mission atrophied in the years since the Soviet Union and Strategic Air Command went out of business...We are definitely focused not only on nuclear (operations) but nuclear deterrence. I think we’ve been able to recreate the same kind of enthusiasm for what we did during the Cold War that kind of drifted away from us ... over the last 15 years... Training for the nuclear mission used to be secondary for bomb-crews, but no more.”

The nuclear mission has been reintroduced to the weapons school, and Elder said he is pushing to have more study of deterrence in professional military education.

“To maintain emphasis on the nuclear mission, a B-52 Wing and a B-2 Squadron will always be designated and in training for nuclear duty, although not on nuclear alert.”

That’s because USAF doesn’t see an urgent threat of attack on the bomber force, and the US isn’t trying to send any other country the message “that we are on a hair trigger, ready to go attack,” Elder explained.”

B-52 Nuclear Bomber

B-47 Nuclear Bomber

Atlas ICBM and Strategic Air Command HQ

Titan ICBM

Minuteman ICBM

CPX Target Plotting

HEADQUARTERS STRATEGIC AIR COMMAND
UNITED STATES AIR FORCE
OFFUTT AIR FORCE BASE, NEBRASKA

15 November 1963

Mr. R. E. Schmaltz
Defense Intelligence Agency
DIAAP-1F1
Washington 25, D. C.

Dear Bob

I have reviewed your Space Study and am happy to say it was very impressive.

I want to commend you on a job well done and express the entire Division's favorable reaction to your study.

Bob, it was a pleasure having you with us for two weeks and I am looking forward to your next visit. Kindest regards --

Sincerely

GEORGE J. KEEGAN, JR.
Colonel, USAF
Chief, Air Estimates Division
Directorate of Intelligence

Strategic Air Command Letter

Personnel File Photo

CERTIFICATE OF RETIREMENT

FROM THE ARMED FORCES OF THE UNITED STATES OF AMERICA

TO ALL WHO SHALL SEE THESE PRESENTS, GREETING:

THIS IS TO CERTIFY THAT

LIEUTENANT COLONEL ROBERT E. SCHMALTZ

HAVING SERVED FAITHFULLY AND HONORABLY

WAS RETIRED FROM THE

UNITED STATES AIR FORCE

ON THE SIXTH DAY OF NOVEMBER

ONE THOUSAND NINE HUNDRED AND EIGHTY-FIVE

SLOAN R. GILL, Major General, USAF
Chief of Air Force Reserve

CHIEF OF STAFF

Certificate of Retirement - USAF

5

Air Target Intelligence 1949-1966

Targeting Background

In December 1942, General Hap Arnold, the Army Air Corp Chief of Staff, signed a directive that led to the formation of the Committee of Operations Analysts (COA). The COA was an agency in the Army Air Corps for the study of strategic bombardment targets. The assimilation of industrial intelligence from all sources and analyses of that information for the purpose of air target selection was the responsibility of the COA. Subcommittees were delegated to study pertinent European industrial systems, transportation systems and military targets. From 1942 to 1949, the COA went through various reorganizations and eventually evolved into three divisions: Air Targeting, Target Materials and Physical Vulnerability. I was in the Target Materials Division.

Air Target Charts

My first job in the Federal Government was as an Industrial Engineer analyzing different industry configurations from a targeting point of view. At the beginning of the Cold War it was discovered that we did not have maps and charts of the Soviet Union. Some of the best maps were National Geographic maps, which were inadequate for bombing target charts.

Libraries had documents on cities, population, industries, etc., that could help develop target charts. Also, German Prisoners of War (POW) in Russia were interrogated and provided much descriptive information on installations from POW Reports. The Germans were obsessed with photoreconnaissance and covered lots of the Soviet Union with stereo aerial photographs. The US captured most of the stereo photographs and held them in the National Archives. These stereo photographs were the basic source to construct our initial target charts for our strategic bombers (we didn't have missiles yet). I was responsible for identifying and plotting industrial and military targets on the bombing charts. I became familiar with all the major cities in the Soviet Union.

Radar Bombing Charts

My second job as an Intelligence Analyst was at a World War II Tempo U building at 12th and Constitution Avenue in Washington DC. The building was a disgrace, but included divisions involved in Air Targeting, Target Materials, and Physical Vulnerability, which developed the first circular slide rule to determine the effects of nuclear weapons. The target charts mentioned above, with the addition of radar returns, became the reference points for developing strategic radar bombing target systems.

The Air Force had developed radar systems that could be used in bombing targets. As intelligence analysts we went to a training school and flew missions where we bombed simulated targets at Mather Air Force Base, California. The charts indicated the radar returns of the target areas. The Air Force had flown missions over Baltimore that generated photographs of radar returns. The intelligence problem was how to depict radar returns of buildings in the Soviet Union on charts to be used for bombing. We accomplished this by estimating the heights and construction materials of the industrial and military installations from stereo photography and converting these too different categories of radar returns. These radar returns were then plotted on target charts for the bombardier to plan the bombing of the targets.

I prepared a set of specifications for constructing radar return charts and taught classes in making these charts at the Aeronautical Chart and Information Center in St. Louis, Missouri and Reconnaissance Technical Squadrons at the U.S. Air Force in Europe. Also, I traveled to military bases in Europe and the Pacific Theater (Hawaii and Japan) to determine the requirements for target materials in the operational units. On a requirements trip to Hawaii on the day it became a state, there was a big celebration in the streets and the Navy bombed the Waikiki Beach with flares.

Missile Target Data Sheets

Another assignment involved preparing Missile Target Data Sheets (MTDS), in coordination with SAC. These were used for missiles as maps were used for bombing. The MTDS was a unique form of target material. Precise geophysical location of the launch site and target had to be identified. This required developing detailed geophysical, geodetic data and orbital calculations for the missiles (GPS wasn't invented yet). The first missile was the ATLAS programmed against the Soviets. An amusing turnaround to the ATLAS missile is that today ATLAS 5 at Cape Kennedy was used for launching US commercial satellites because the Russian engines were cheaper. The Russians used many small kerosene boosters where the US used a liquid hydrogen engine.

Security

When the Air Force Intelligence was integrated into the Defense Intelligence Agency I ended up in the DIA Plans Office, which involved a lot of paper pushing.

I felt that I spent too many years in the intelligence business – 17 years. When you work in the classified intelligence environment you live in a different world. It was exciting work during the Cold War. I had one unpleasant experience. Some of my work required special clearances above Top Secret.

When I first went into the business, I had to fill out a form that wanted to know if I had any relatives overseas. I didn't know of any and asked my parents if I had any. I put some names down. Years later, when they processed my application for a higher clearance, they noticed my relatives overseas and that my mother-in-law came from Schmalkalten Germany and her next-door neighbor spoke broken English. As a result, I became a prime suspect. It just happens that Schmalkalten was located in the middle of the Fulda Gap area in Germany where everyone figured that was where the Soviets would invade to the Rhine and World War III would start.

All simulation models, including my own discussed later, had the Russians attacking through the Fulda Gap. In addition, with a name like Schmaltz, my parents told me to list their nationality as Polish. (It is amusing that I was in the service in World War II and the Reserves and my father escaped from his home to come to this country so he wouldn't be drafted by the Russian Czar.) With all that suspicious background, my special clearance was held up for a few years and was a very painful period of my life.

Finally, a colonel I worked for had a general write a letter about me and that I was "o.k." (It took a general officer). Then I had to take a lie detector test to prove that I wasn't a spy. The examining officer would only talk of my mother-in-law coming from Schmalkalten and for me to locate it on a map. I didn't know where it was at the time. I passed the lie detector test and was granted the special clearances. It was a humiliating and depressing experience that affected my family and me for many years.

As I mentioned before, I grew up in Scranton, PA and worked in the Washington, DC area. I always thought my ancestors came from Germany. Recently, I did the genealogy research on my Schmaltz relatives. I couldn't prove any German background back to the 1970s. (I did learn that my last name was spelled wrong – without a "t').

In the 19th century there were a lot of wars and revolutions, and Napoleon was in Germany. This caused a lot of the German population to immigrate to Poland/Prussia where Catherine the Great was trying to develop the land between Germany and Russia. My grandfather settled in southern Poland, which was occupied four times by Poland, Germany, Russia and the Ukraine. The Czar of Russia was drafting all the men for his Army. My grandfather was wealthy and sent his four sons, including my father, to America. He stayed behind and later was sent with my grandmother in a cattle car train to Siberia where they died. My father settled in Scranton PA. My military, active, reserve and civilian experience seemed strange to my father since he was a draft dodger from the Czar's Russian Army.

Air Targets Association

The people who worked in Targets (since 1949) formed an association of Target employees. They meet twice a year at Ft. Myers for lunch. However, there are a few of us left. K.T. Johnson, the president, and Jo Lovejoy, the secretary, have kept it alive. K.T. wrote the following in the Target Association Newsletter:

> "There is something special about the era in which we worked together and what it has meant to our group. It is remarkable that we are still meeting together on a regular basis. We had a specific, common, and important mission --- targeting. We were able to see our finished product (target intelligence) incorporated into US war plans. Although our specific areas of expertise were different, we were unified in producing target materials, target jackets, maintaining the BE, the TDI, and CTIF and special target studies. We cut our targeting teeth in an era of paucity of information. It was a unique time and situation that will never again be repeated because of the advances that have been made in technology and the fact that the major adversary's capabilities have dramatically diminished. We were faced with the daunting task of building a target database with very little information. Before the advent, in later years, of a prodigious amount of overhead photography, we were challenged to think...how to

combine bits and pieces of information, much of it low level, with available COMINT and finally produce intelligence at the SECRET level useful to the planners. This requirement to think, to share and to debate knit us into a team that created loyalty, respect and professional pride in ourselves and in each other that exists to this day."

General Hap Arnold

Business Trip – When Hawaii Became a State

6

The Space Race

Background

Space capabilities: Space systems, in principle, can acquire and distribute information about adversaries' preparations for and initiation of attacks, about the weather affecting military operations, and much more. An aggressor would have large incentives to attack them. The US needs military satellite systems that will continue to function or can at least be reconstituted speedily, not only in peacetime, but also to support our forces in resisting attack by Soviet land, sea and air forces.

The space race was a race between the Soviets and the US in achievements, applications and exploration in space with satellites and humans. Sputnik 1, the Soviet satellite, was the first satellite and was launched on 4 October 1957. The technology was important because of its military applications and reputation. I was in the intelligence business at the time and not only the people in the US, but a lot of people around the world became concerned.

The US launched its first satellite - Explorer 1 - four months later. Both countries expanded their space programs and the race was on.

Soviet Cosmonauts

Soviet Cosmonaut Yuri Gagarin was the first human to go into orbital space in the Soviet Union's Vostok 1 Spacecraft on April 12, 1961. He was in orbit for 108 minutes. He had no control over his spacecraft and his reentry was controlled by a computer program. He ejected after re-entry into the earth's atmosphere at an altitude of 20,000 feet and landed by parachute. He proved that man could endure the rigors of lift off, reentry and weightlessness. Colonel Gagarin died on March 27, 1968 when the MIG-15 airplane he was piloting crashed near Moscow. See his photo at the end of this chapter.

Cosmonaut Gherman Titov was the second man to go into orbital fight on 6 August 1961. The flight objectives were to investigate the human effects and ability to work after a prolong weightlessness flight in orbit and subsequent return to earth. After 17.5 orbits, the spacecraft reentered on August 7, 1961 and made a parachute landing after riding his ejection seat out of the capsule. I met Titov, something I will discuss at the end of this chapter.

John Glenn was the first US man to go into orbit on February 20, 1962. Everyone was worried about the US-Soviet Space Race. There are two charts at the end of this chapter showing the period from 1957 to 1987: the "US vs. Soviet Space Launches" and "US vs. Soviet Operational Satellites in Orbit."

Space Studies

Later on, I became Chief of the Soviet Space Branch in the DIA. I prepared a study that estimated the Soviet Space Systems and capabilities for the next 5 years. The study was used as the basic reference point for the first National Intelligence Estimate (NIE) on the Soviet Space Program.

On a Reserve tour at the Assistant Chief of Staff (ACS) Intelligence in the Pentagon, I prepared a report on the intelligence requirements for space stations. This was at the beginning of the space programs. The report was secret and I submitted it to the ACS Intelligence, who forwarded it to the Space Office. Months later, as part of my civilian intelligence job, I requested a copy of my reserve study and was told that it was highly classified and that I couldn't see it.

I also had a big failure during an analysis of a photo in Cuba where I discovered three large circular installations that looked like and could be radar antennas. These could be used to command satellite actions against the US. (This concept in Cuba was covered in a recent James Bond Movie.)

After consulting with technical radar experts, I prepared a report and started coordinating it up the decision-making line. The report got to the Secretary of Defense level, when it was discovered by CIA that my three radar antennas were rainwater collectors. I quietly destroyed the report.

A more successful report was when I analyzed the threat of Soviet satellites against Strategic Air Command (SAC) Airfields and bombers. SAC was always concerned about the survival of their aircraft on their airfields. I discovered that if you plot the orbit tracks of the Soviet reconnaissance satellites against the SAC air bases, there was a definite logic in determining the location of the bomber force. You could either disperse the force or take other actions to protect the force. Later, I briefed the Director of Intelligence at HQ Strategic Air Command, Estimates Division, Omaha, Nebraska, where it was well received.

I was fortunate to meet Soviet Cosmonaut Gherman Titov at the US State Department in Washington, DC, at the Third International Space Science Symposium. The pictures at the end of this chapter show Titov and Astronaut John Glenn at the symposium.

Space was a popular topic in the sixties. Independent of my work, I established a Space Explorer Post for teenage boys. Explorer Posts in the sixties were started to extend the Boy Scout organization for older boys to concentrate on a specific topic, such as space.

Astronaut John Glenn was very interested in the space explorer effort and sent me a complimentary letter. See it at the end of this chapter.

US vs. Soviet Operational Satellites in Orbit

Since the early 1970s, the Soviet Union has kept more satellites in orbit than the United States. At least ninety percent of Soviet satellites and about two-thirds of US satellites have military roles. The Soviets now have twice as many military satellites in orbit as the US has. This Soviet proliferation would help keep their satellite systems operating while under attack in wartime.

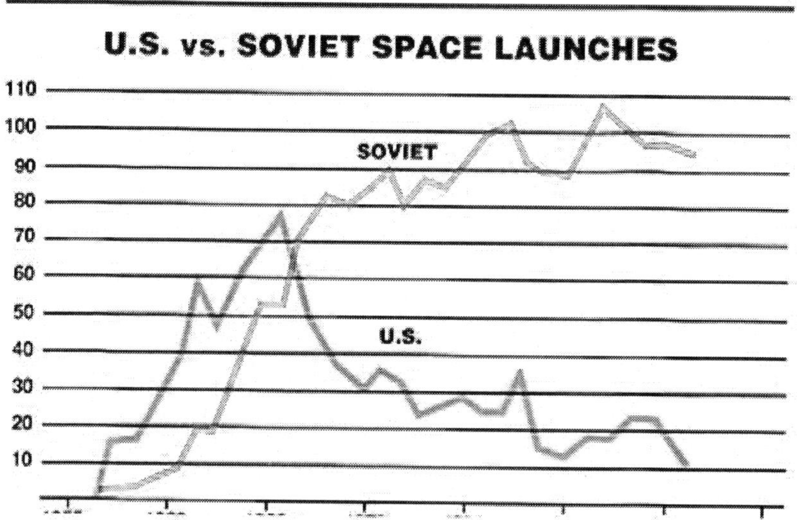

US vs. Soviet Space Launches

Launch capability is another important way to enable a satellite system to operate in wartime. For two decades the frequency of Soviet space launches, as well as their payload weight to orbit (not shown) far exceeded that of the US.

Soviet Cosmonaut Yuri Gagarin

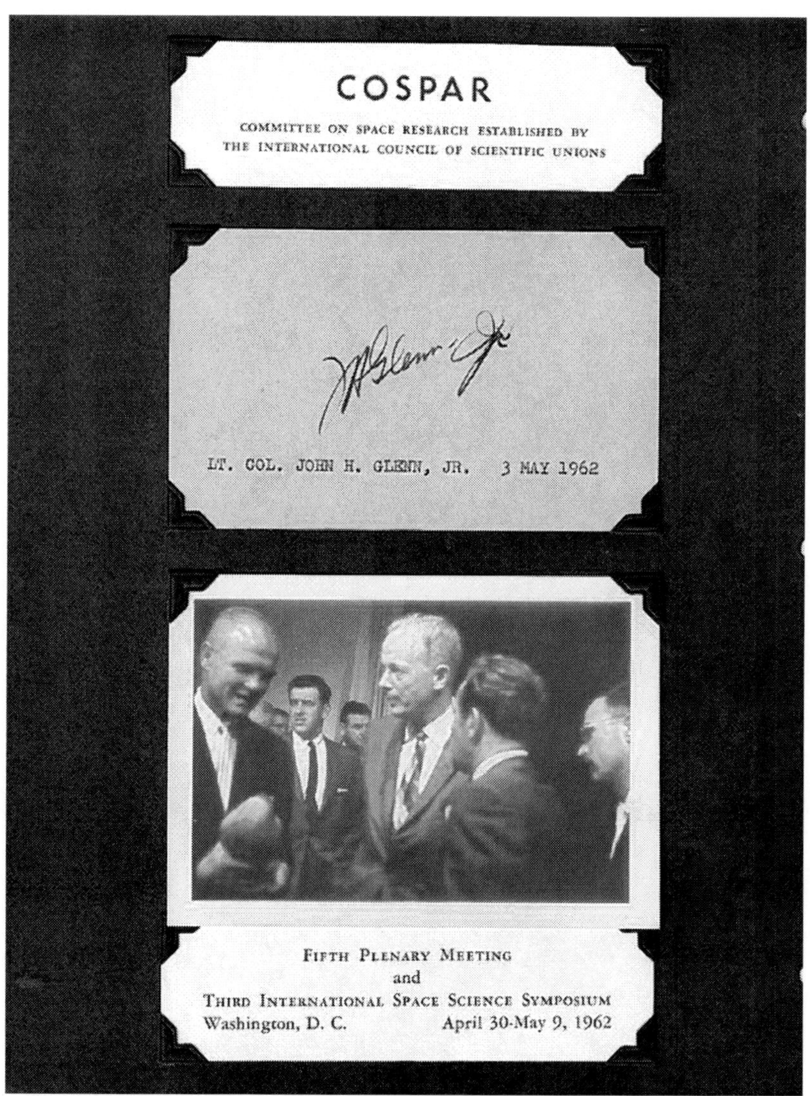

COSPAR International Space Science Symposium

Cosmonaut Gherman Titov (top photo) and Astronaut John Glenn (bottom photo)

Cosmonaut Titov Entering US State Department

203 Sleepy Hollow Court
Seabrook, Texas
November 26, 1965

Mr. Robert E. Schmaltz
6708 Dean Drive
McLean, Virginia

Dear Mr. Schmaltz:

Thank you very much for your kind letter of October 20th and I regret I was traveling in Europe for an extended period when your letter arrived.

It sounds as though you have a most active program and you are certainly to be complimented for it. I do not know when I will be getting to the Washington area again or when we might catch an evening together, but I will certainly keep this in mind and keep your phone number and hope that we can get together one of these times for a question and answer session or whatever you and your other members would like to discuss. Getting an organization such as this under-way and setting up an active program as you have is certainly a big job and I wish you every success.

Thanks again for the invitation, and although I cannot set a time, perhaps we will be able to get together sometime in the future.

Sincerely yours,

J H Glenn, Jr.

John H. Glenn, Jr.
Colonel, USMC (Ret.)
NASA Astronaut

Glad to hear you have the Space Explorer Post under-way, and look forward to seeing you one of these days —

JHG Jr.

Personal Letter from Astronaut John Glenn

7

Systems Analysis Whiz Kids 1966 – 1978

Background

In the early 60s, President Kennedy selected Robert McNamara as the Secretary of Defense. He had been President of the Ford Motor Company and had extensive operations research experience during World War II. McNamara set up a group of people called the Whiz Kids (similar to that which he had at Ford) to monitor the military policies and weapon system acquisitions. They produced controversial studies and had a low popularity with the military because of the way the Whiz Kids treated the military personnel with their controversial studies and attitude. Systems analysis became the buzzwords, the way decisions were quantitatively rationalized inside the Pentagon.

To counter this attack against the military, each service set up a Systems Analysis Office of highly educated military and civilian personnel. In the Air Force the office was Assistant Chief of Staff, Studies and Analysis (AF/SA). It was commanded by Major General Howard Davis and was the Air Force's answer to Dr. Alain Enthoven who was Assistant Secretary of Defense for Systems Analysis (and his Whiz kids) who demanded answers regarding force structures, levels, and weapon system mixes.

French Air Bases

I joined AF/SA in 1966. In the 60s, General Charles de Gaulle, President of France, was not too happy with a military organization between the North Atlantic Treaty Organization (NATO) and the US. He thought that the US in a nuclear war would be more interested in defending Washington than Paris. Therefore, he decided not to form an organization with the US and NATO, but instead to form his own French military arsenal. This resulted in the removal of all foreign air bases and troops from France.

My first assignment in AF/SA was as a Senior Operations Research Analyst on a team to restructure the Air Force base structure and forces throughout Europe. We developed a matrix of each Air Base verses their characteristics, etc. Then we weighted the values for each base we summed up their values, and developed some base structure options. We developed a briefing of the options for the decision makers. The study was used as a basis to relocate our air bases in Europe.

Saber Measures

Major General Glenn Kent, the Assistant Chief of Staff for Studies and Analysis thought we were concentrating a lot of our analysis on computers. That was in the 60s. Amusingly, today – in 2008, I read that the present Secretary of Defense, Robert Gates had a similar comment on the use of computers in the analytic process. General Kent suggested we examine historical data as an analytical tool. As a result, a study group was formed called SABER MEASURES with me as the director.

Part of the problem at that time in the Air Force was articulating the Air Interdiction Mission to the Defense Department Whiz Kids. They wanted to abolish the mission. Many studies were prepared on the effectiveness of Air Interdiction based on both US and German historical data. One was to determine the role interdiction played in the breakout from the ground stalemate on entering Rome. Another was on the German General's debate on the effectiveness of interdiction to delay the transfer of German Armies during the Normandy Invasion.

Much of the historical data was German sources collected by Trevor Dupuy and his Dupuy Institute. He was a top military historian who testified before Congress on various military matters and wrote the Military Historical Encyclopedia. He was my contractor and one of his tasks was to organize the historical air interdiction data into combat equations. These became a series of equations that developed into the QJM Model – Quantitative Judgment Model. This model, based on historical data could be used to determine battle outcomes. It was used as a background to support the TAC Interdictor Model discussed below.

TAC Interdictor

This model simulated all the Soviet forces, logistics and transportation in West Germany for an attack thru the Fulda Gap to the Rhine River, and the air attacks from air bases in Europe. The simulation was very detailed and included the major highways, rail lines, bridges, supply depots, firepower vehicles, convoys, logistics intelligence weather, air operations, defenses, a priority daily target system, etc. The ground battles generated losses and as the forces were re-supplied, the fighters attacked the convoys. The outputs of the model generated effectiveness curves that were used as inputs to an overall Tactical Air Operations model, which was used for the sizing of tactical air forces.

Theoretically, all the services were to determine their military requirements and size their own forces, but actually the force sizing studies they did were modified by the Defense Department Systems Analysis and Congress. If a congressman wanted so many planes placed in the budget, it would be added.

TAC Avenger

In the 60s, the Air Force proposed to develop an air superiority fighter aircraft – an FX – for the 70s and later. Our assignment was to develop a realistic technique that would let the Air Force predict, with computers, the outcome of battles in the sky between two given aircraft such as the F-4 and the Soviet MIG-21. Basically, our team was to develop a computer simulation model for a new fighter plane. The team included Colonel Charleson, Major Lamb and a contractor.

We decided to structure the model from an existing model, an F-100 model. The new model would support the justification for the F-15 fighter. It would simulate the aircraft's weapons (guns and missiles), avionics and energy maneuverability, including the pilot's decision-making procedures. The TAC AVENGER Model was to simulate flying in three dimensions and using a decision tree to simulate the pilot's actions in various conditions. According to Major General Kent and Major Garey, when we briefed them on the model, this was the first model that simulated flying in three dimensions. They had been using a two dimensional model at Wright-Patterson AFB.

We developed the pilot's actions by conducting surveys and discussions with fighter pilots at different Air Force bases and at the Fighter Weapons Center at Nellis AFB, Las Vegas, Nevada. Two fighter pilots joined the team who should be mentioned here. The first is Major Larry

Welch and Major Kurt Haderly. Haderly was a dedicated fighter pilot who made some major contributions to the model development and eventually went to NASA Space Flight Center to become an astronaut. He was killed when his glove came off in a high altitude flight.

The second fighter pilot is worth a special story. I asked him to check out the weapon simulation program in the model. Larry came to us straight out of the cockpit of a fighter. He knew nothing about computers and simulations and looked at us in a strange way when we told him how the model flies in a dogfight. He didn't have a degree and when I asked him if he could come in on Sunday to work he said he couldn't because he taught Sunday school.

Larry eventually got a BS and an MS degree and learned more about the model than anyone else. He got his own team of pilots to expand, update and operate the model. He briefed the model throughout the Air Force, Defense Department and Congress to sell the F-15. He became a general, ended up as a four-star general and became the Chief of Staff of the Air Force. After he retired he became Head of the Joint Chiefs' Institute of Defense Analysis and was on various Defense Commissions. He turned out to be the finest and most competent General Officer I knew and reminded me of World War II General Marshall.

This page intentionally left blank.

Dogfight Portrayal. The TAC Avenger Group briefed and provided information on the model to Claude Witze, Sr. Editor of Air Force Magazine. He wrote an article for Air Force Magazine (January 1968), which included a good description and graphic of the model as follows (See the figure Dogfight Portrayal at end of this chapter.):

> "The Dogfight Portrayal shown is typical of conflict in North Viet Nam. MIG-21is vectored for tail attack on USAF F-4. This common situation provides the basis for TAC AVENGER to simulate combat with computers. The tactical situation is described to the computer, along with data on what the MIG-21 and F-4 can do when pressed for top performance. The computer also absorbs full outlines of possible fighter maneuvers, plus logic used by USAF pilots when flying them. Printout display output from the computer in both numerical and graphic forms are generated. A horizontal profile shows the path of fighters as viewed overhead. A vertical profile shows altitudes achieved in battle ... Numerical outputs are produced as aircraft maneuvers and are depicted in the Dog Fight Portrayal graphic. There the F-4 makes a tight turn to evade a missile launched by a MIG-21 and tries to get the enemy off his tail into vertical pursuit and goes on, almost straight up, to achieve victory in the air."

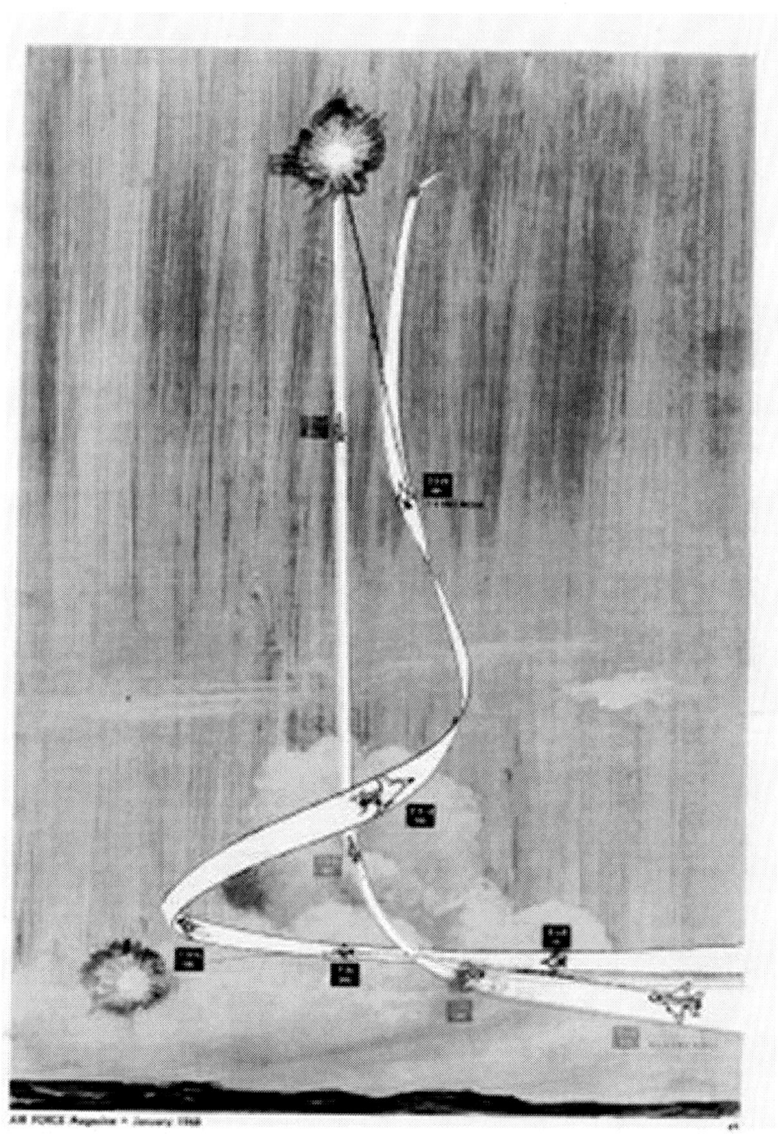

TAC Avenger Dogfight Portrayal

Headquarters U.S. Air Force Operations Research Analyst.

Outline on map in background covers the area in Germany of my Tactical Air Interdiction Simulation Model where we expected the Soviets to start World War III.

Retirement Ceremony

Department of the Air Force

CERTIFICATE OF SERVICE

Robert E. Schmaltz

In recognition of 31 *years of faithful and devoted Federal Service on the occasion of retirement from civilian employment*

30 June 1978
DATE

Air Force Civilian Certificate of Service

HQ OPERATING INSTRUCTION
NO. 28-5

HEADQUARTERS U. S. AIR FORCE
Washington, 4 *February 1966*

War Planning and Studies

AIR FORCE STUDIES

This instruction defines and states the objectives of Air Force studies; assigns responsibilities; provides guidance for the formulation and accomplishment of studies by the Air Staff; and directs procedures for monitoring and reviewing designated studies. Other pertinent references are AFM 10-4, HOI 10-8, and HOI 11-53.

---

1. The Significance of Studies. A substantial portion of Air Staff effort is directed toward the accomplishment of studies. These studies have a significant impact on the roles and missions, make-up and character, and the effectiveness of the future United States Air Force and on concepts for employment of air power. In view of the resources involved and the impact of the over-all study program on the future Air Force, it is extremely important that studies be efficiently and effectively accomplished on a timely basis.

2. Definition and Objective of Air Force Studies:

a. *Definition of a Study.* A study is an orderly effort to identify and evaluate feasible solutions to a problem or reasonable alternatives for decision on an issue. A study is characterized by a systematic identification of data, facts and information relevant to the problem or issue and the application of logical analytical processes to these factors.

b. *Objective of a Study.* The objective of a study is to develop improved understanding of a problem or issue by clearly showing the effects of, and interrelationships among, the relevant factors. Study efforts are not a substitute for responsible judgment and decisions. Their purpose is to nourish the wisdom of the decision maker by providing a clear, complete, and objective basis on which to exercise his judgment in arriving at an appropriate decision.

3. Classes of Air Staff Studies. For purposes of this HOI, studies are grouped into the following two principal categories:

a. *Designated Studies:*

(1) These studies are approved and so designated by the Chief of Staff. They will normally be the most important, highest priority studies of the greatest significance to the Air Force, DOD, and the Nation. This class may include studies:

(a) Directed upon the Air Force by OSD and OSAF.

(b) Directed by the Chief of Staff or the Vice Chief of Staff, and those

(c) Otherwise so designated by the Chief of Staff or the Vice Chief of Staff, to include those proposed by the Deputy Chiefs of Staff.

(2) Designated Studies will be limited in number and given precedence over other

---

This instruction supersedes HOI 10-12, 27 May 1965.

studies in the allocation of resources for their accomplishment. Studies in this class will comprise the Designated Study Program. The guidance and procedures outlined in this instruction for the conduct, content, and review of studies are directive for this class of studies.

b. *Functional Studies.* These studies include those conducted in the Air Staff that are not classified as Designated Studies. This class comprises the majority of Air Staff study efforts and has a significant impact on normal staff work accomplished in the functional staff agencies. Conduct of studies in this class is the day-to-day responsibility of the functional staff and the guidance and procedures of this instruction are not mandatory. A DCS may determine from time to time that a study in this class, over which he has cognizance, should be classified as a Designated Study. In such cases action will be taken to have the study so designated and approved by the Chief of Staff, whereupon the procedures of this instruction become directive.

4. Responsibilities for the Study Program:

a. *The Chief of Staff* will:

(1) Approve those studies which are to be Designated Studies.

(2) Approve study objectives and terms of reference for Designated Studies.

(3) Assign the OPR on all Designated Studies.

(4) Require periodic progress reports on the accomplishment of Designated Studies.

(5) Approve the individual study plans, the Designated Study Program and changes to both.

b. *Deputy Chiefs of Staff.* Each Deputy Chief of Staff will:

(1) Advise the Chief of Staff on requirements for Designated Studies. Proposals for candidate studies should be submitted in the format shown in attachment 2.

(2) Function as OPR for those Designated Studies assigned by the Chief of Staff. (See figure 3, attachment 1, for Designated Study flow when the OPR is other than the DCS/P&O.) When designated as OPR, a DCS will:

(a) Furnish a qualified study leader and provide working level support.

(b) With the assistance and collaboration of the Chief of Operations Analysis:

1. Prepare the initial study plan.

2. Establish procedures for continuing review and monitoring of the study.

(c) Assure accomplishment of the study under the guidance specified in the study plan.

(d) Prepare progress reports and documentation as required.

(e) Provide study effort, working-level support, and assistance in accomplishing both Designated and functional studies.

c. *The Deputy Chief of Staff, Plans and Operations* will supervise and direct the Directorate of Studies and Analysis which is a HQ USAF field extension. (See Figure 2, attachment 1, for Designated Study flow when the DCS/P&O is OPR.)

d. *The Director of Studies and Analysis* will:

(1) Formulate, in conjunction with other staff offices, a Designated Studies Program for review by the Air Force Council and recommendation to the Chief of Staff for approval. (See Figure 1, attachment 1, for flow of the Designated Studies Program.)

(2) Conduct, or assist in conducting all Designated Studies.

(3) Assist in preparing study plans for functional studies.

(4) Provide a study library service for the Air Staff which will include:

(a) A consolidated cross-reference file of Designated and functional studies.

(b) Reference material on other Air Force studies, both in-house and contract, and on studies of other Government departments and agencies which may be relevant to the Air Staff Study Program.

(c) Library research service in support of Air Force studies.

e. *The Chief, Operations Analysis* will:

(1) Make recommendations to the Chief of Staff on the statement of study objectives and terms of reference for Designated Studies.

(2) Assist the OPR study leader in the preparation of the initial study plan for each Designated Study.

(3) Conduct reviews of Designated Study plans, and make recommendations to the Chief of Staff as deemed appropriate.

(4) Maintain continuous review of progress during accomplishment of Designated Studies and keep the Chief of Staff advised of:

(a) Study progress and the analytical quality of the study.

(b) Continuing responsiveness to the study objectives and terms of reference.

(5) Provide study personnel to assist in accomplishing both Designated Studies and, within capabilities, functional studies.

(6) Prepare for the use of the Secretary of the Air Force and the Chief of Staff an evaluative appraisal of study quality and responsiveness to study objectives on all Designated Studies.

(7) Act as adviser to the Chief of Staff and the Air Staff on the overall studies program.

5. Conduct and Review of Designated Studies:

a. *Study Plan.* The first step in the conduct of a Designated Study will be to prepare a written initial study plan. The plan will include:

(1) A clear and comprehensive statement of the problem.

(2) A Statement of Relevance which will explain how the problem or issue being studied bears on decisions and how they, in turn, affect USAF effectiveness.

(3) An outline of the logical structure of the over-all study, with identification of the basic analytical methodology that will be used.

(4) Identification of criteria against which solutions and alternatives will be evaluated and compared.

(5) Identification of factual material to be used in conducting current studies, and of past studies which have a clear bearing on the problem.

(6) A systematic breakdown of the basic study into subquestions which will be studied individually. This breakdown will include a clear indication of how the results of each of these substudies will be integrated into the overall study.

(7) A list of relevant independent topics that will be explored separately until their exact relation to the main issue can be fully appreciated.

(8) A Study Resources Requirements Estimate, on a time-phased schedule of the resources, including manpower, TDY expenditures, administrative support, and office space required to complete the study. The proposed sources of such resources, to include major command and AF contractual sources such as RAND, will be specified wherever possible. Timing of progress reports will be indicated.

b. *Study Content and Accomplishment.* Content and accomplishment of the study and the study plan will be kept consistent. Periodic amendment of the plan may be required as the study effort proceeds. Proposed amendments will be reviewed and approved by procedures established during review and approval of the initial study plan. To the extent possible, factors relevant to the study will be characterized in quantitative terms and the logical processes will be mathematical. Qualitative factors will be treated with correspondingly rigorous logic. The study will clearly show the alternatives available for judgmental choice and will include an objective appraisal of the probable impact of each alternative.

c. *Reports and Documentation.* A written report of the completed study will be prepared under the general guidance in AFM 10-4 and HOI 10-8, as specifically modified herein. The report will include the initial study plan, and all amendments to it, and a summary, not over two pages in length, of the entire study. A separate Concluding Statement of Relevance will be prepared by the OPR to provide an appraisal of how the study results bear on decision problems in the context of the initial Statement of Relevance of the Study Plan. Recommendations for future study may be made when considered appropriate. However, the content of the study will not contain recommendations for selection of a particular alternative nor for a specific course of action. This limitation does not preclude the study chairman, a Director or DCS with OPR responsibility, AFCOA, the Air Staff Board, or the Air Force Council from making recommendations to the Chief of Staff. However, these recommendations will be separate from the study content and will normally be included in a cover letter to the study. The letter transmitting a study report to higher authority will contain the decision or recommendations of the Chief of Staff.

d. *Review and Approval.* Designated Studies will be continually reviewed and monitored by the Office of the Chief of Staff from their initiation to completion. The initial study plan will be reviewed and approved by the Office of the Chief of Staff, at which time procedures for review and approval of amendments to the study plan will be specified. The study plan (as amended) will be used as a guide for the continuing review process during study accomplishment and for review of the completed study. When appropriate, the OPR will sponsor

Designated Studies for review by the Air Staff Board under procedures prescribed in HOI 21-18. In these cases, the Air Staff Board will make any recommendations it considers appropriate to the Air Force Council. The Air Force Council normally will review Designated Studies and submit recommendations to the Chief of Staff.

e. *Supplemental Information on Interstaff Procedures:*

(1) Paragraphs 4 and 5 outline and assign basic responsibilities for accomplishing Air Force studies. Attachment 1 supplements these instructions by portraying graphically and in detail the important sequential steps required to accomplish assigned responsibilities, both for the Designated Studies Program and the individual Designated Study. The interface between the separate staff agencies most actively involved in the development of Air Force studies is also shown.

(a) *The Designated Studies Program.* The process of developing the Designated Studies Program is shown in figure 1. The chart depicts, along the left side, those staff agencies most actively involved in the program formulation. Required steps are shown across the top of the chart, and sequential actions are reflected by the flow diagram. An explanation is included for each action indicated.

(b) *Individual Designated Studies.* Development of the individual Designated Study is shown in figures 2 and 3 as two separate cases: When OPR is DCS/P&O (figure 2), and when OPR is other than DCS/P&O (figure 3). Action agencies, required steps, and sequential actions are portrayed by flow diagrams (see e(1)(a), above). A full explanation of indicated actions is provided.

(2) Attachment 2, "Format for a Study Proposal," is to be used when recommending candidate studies for approval as Designated Studies (see paragraph 4b(1)). This format is self-explanatory. The information required is considered the minimum necessary for adequate review and appraisal of a study proposal.

(3) The above procedures are not mandatory for *functional studies.* However, when practicable, functional studies should follow closely these lines of coordination and actions in the interest of achieving the highest quality results.

FOR THE CHIEF OF STAFF

OFFICIAL

R. J. PUGH
Colonel, USAF
Director of Administrative Services

HEWITT T. WHELESS
Lieutenant General, U. S. Air Force
Assistant Vice Chief of Staff

2 Attachments
1. Flow Charts (Figures 1, 2, and 3)
2. Study Proposal Format

Air Force Studies Operating Instruction (4)

8
Consulting 1979-2004

Retirement

After 30 years working in the Pentagon and Washington, I moved and retired to Vermont in 1978 to cleanse my soul. When you're young in Washington it is exciting to work there, but after 30 years it was different, and with the heat, humidity, politics, and pollution all summer it was not much fun. In Vermont I had 10 acres on top of a mountain in the ski area and planned to build my home, go skiing, play golf and enjoy life.

After the first year, I talked to the President of the Power Company that was one of the largest companies in Vermont. He offered me a job to do a study on the potential of hydroelectric power sites on the rivers in Vermont. This didn't appeal to me so I thought I would try something part time in the Boston area around Hanscom Air Force Base.

I took a part-time job with Systems Architect in Lexington, MA. I led a group to prepare a report on the compatibility of existing Air Force systems with systems under development to determine their interoperability. I worked two days a week and was able to take work home with me. This was a good arrangement. Unfortunately, the president of the company was arrested for not paying the employees' Social Security payments to the IRS. The company had no future.

RJO

Later, I worked for a company called RJO under contract with the Air Force. This was an interesting and challenging job where a co-worker and I prepared a study on the future investment strategy for the Developing Planning Office, Electronic Systems Department, Hanscom AFB. The study was a strategy for inputs to the Command Control Mission Plan and included concepts of the future within Air Force Systems Command. It was a plan for future ESD system projects for the next 5 years. Our effort produced a study: "C31 Developing Planning and Investment Strategy for Electronic Systems Division," September 30, 1988.

Planning Research Corporation (PRC)

The start of this consulting job was a bit unusual. I was chopping wood one day in Vermont when someone from New Jersey named Moose from Planning Research Corporation called and wanted me to come down to New Jersey for an interview. After many refusals, I agreed to go for the interview during a snowstorm. When I arrived late in the day, I was met by all the division chiefs around a table with a stack of documents - and presented with a problem to be solved in one day (this was my interview).

I thought that they were a strange group of people. They were on the verge of losing a $4 million contract for lack of analytical support. I took the one-foot of documents back to the hotel. After a few scotches, I reviewed them. I went back to my audience the next day and recommended an approach. This turned out to be the analytical methodology used in conducting tests in the Joint Interoperability of Tactical Command and Control (JINTACCS) Intelligence Program. The approach was used by the military services to measure the compatibility and interoperability for the exchange of information between communication centers. After this experience I had a 20-year working relationship with Moose (Francesco Musorrafiti).

Engineering and Professional Services (EPS)

Moose left PRC and started his own company, EPS. There was one employee – Moose who had help from his daughter as secretary. Today he has 450 employees worldwide. One day he invited me to lunch. I went to his office and he asked me to sit down and write a proposal – no lunch. After his company started to operate, I continued to do part-time consulting. The arrangement was that I could spend a few days in the New Jersey office and do the rest of the work at my home in Vermont.

One day as I was leaving to go home he asked me to write a proposal for the US Army in Germany, which I did. He got the contract and my wife and I spent the next year and a half in Heidelberg Germany consulting with HQ US Army Europe (USAREUR). The contract was to conduct a study of the Army information systems – computer and communication systems - what and where they were and how they interoperated with each other and the other services. I would work a week in Heidelberg, go sightseeing in Europe for a week, then go home and work for two weeks. Then I would return to Germany the next month.

I went through this same routine for a year and a half. This was the highlight of my working career and included extensive traveling with my wife. As I look back at this experience, there is no way you could plan anything like this. It just happened.

The final study was "USAREUR C3I System Interoperability Study, Integration and Interoperability Analysis," September 1985. Basically, the study involved a survey of all the communication and computer systems, how they operated between units, and problems involved. It was used by the DCS/Information Management, HQ, USAREUR and as inputs to information system architecture studies.

I continued consulting with EPS part-time. Some of the studies I did were:

1. “Cost/Schedule Status Report, EPS” August 1987. The C/SSR System was designed to provide management with the framework to organize, plan, direct and control program activity. It was for the USN SATCOM Signal Analyzer Program.

2. “U.S. Army Reserve, Special Operations Study, Data Base Management System,” September 1990.

3. “U.S. Army Reserve, Special Operations Forces Study Plan,” October 1989. It was an approach to analyze personnel resources, logistics systems, command and control, structure school quota management, and training capabilities.

My final assignment with EPS was as the Proposal Manager for a proposal on the “Saudi Arabia Command and Control System.” This involved 10 companies (EPS was the system integrator). After this, I planned to completely retire, commune with Mozart, travel on cruises (60), read, play golf and see my family.

Engineering and Professional Services

9

Some Final Notes

Overall Comments

Overall, my career with the Air Force was interesting and at times, exciting. The day I retired from the Air Force in 1978, I was the Senior Civilian of Air Force Doctrine for one day due to a reorganization of the Air Staff. The next day I retired. I was very lucky in World War II and in the Reserve.

Computer Models

After many years of experience with computer simulation models, I have concluded that they are not reliable outputs for major decisions. Two good examples are predicting the current financial meltdown and global warming. A lot of neat numbers and graphs are generated, but the model is basically compiled by subjective opinions or hazy logic. I learned in life that there are two things you cannot predict – human behavior and the weather. Computer models are based on subjective data, usually biased. When the computers generate neat numbers and curves or when someone says "the computer says," be skeptical.

1945 Christmas Party

In December 1945, the family got together for a Christmas party in Washington, DC. The photo at the end of this chapter shows Herman Eilts, my youngest sister Martha, John Becker, my friend, Elsie, my sister, myself, and my oldest sister Hilda. Hilda became the Administrative Assistant to the Secretary of the Smithsonian Institution in Washington, DC; my sister Elsie was a secretary to the Inspector General of the US Air Force; my sister Martha was a flight nurse who flew Med Evac Missions for the wounded in most of the major battles in the Pacific Theater during World War II. Herman Eilts, who I believe was in Army Intelligence, became the Ambassador to Egypt and worked with Henry Kissinger on the Arab-Israeli Peace Treaty. Herman and I were in Boy Scouts together in Scranton. He was very smart and a good leader. For some reason, I remember one incident with him. We were playing in a gas station when he took a gas hose and poured gas all over me. They washed me off. I mentioned this to him a few years ago but he did not remember it. He was a good ambassador in Egypt.

HealthMedNet

In addition to the work discussed in this book, I developed a Directory of Medical Directories on the Internet (healthmednet.com) and categorized them by 90,000 illness and disease URL/Links. It is the largest such directory on the Internet and is an international brand name.

Even though my sons don't believe it is a good idea i.e., integrate all the good medical directories on the Internet and organize it by illness and disease type, I still believe it was a good idea. When you want some information on an illness or disease, instead of going to Google and getting a lot of garbage, you go to healthmednet.com and you get a list of the good URL/Links on your illness or disease. This was a hobby for me; I didn't have the capital to develop it nor was I interested in the marketing aspect.

Plane Crash

The Pentagon was built during the early years of World War II. There were approximately 23,000 employees. On September 11, 2001 American Airlines Flight 77 crashed into the Pentagon, the US military headquarters, killing 184 people after it was hijacked as part of an al-Qaeda plot. The crash came shortly after two other high-jacked airlines were flown into the twin towers at the World Trade Center in New York. The events remind us of why the US launched its global "war on terror."

The plane crashed in the Pentagon in the area of Ring 1E400. My old office was in the next area, Ring 1D300. See the picture of the crash at the end of this chapter.

A Directory of Illness and Disease URL Directories

Version 5.0 - 90,000 URLs

URL DIRECTORY

11131

HealthMedNet (HMN) Content Service helps individuals and organizations increase their understanding of illnesses and diseases.

HMN is based on the Internet Illness and Disease URL Directory Database, which contains 90,000 illness and disease URL/Links and is updated periodically. It is unique in that it specializes only in illness & disease URL information and includes the names and URLs of select directories and lists, categorized by illness/disease names. The users merely click on the URL/Links that corresponds to the name of their illness or disease to access the Web Page information. See: URL DIRECTORY

HMNservice focuses on organizing, aggregating, and providing illness & disease URL/Links to individual patients, nurses, doctors, medical school students, universities, senior citizens, insurance companies, libraries, and others, such as military and civilian personnel assigned overseas.

Sources of the illness and disease URL information on the Internet include university medical centers, government health departments, health industry sites, medical institutes, medical clinics, Portals, medical professional organizations, clearinghouses, individual health Web Pages, and interactive physicians online.

℞

http://healthmednet.com/ 3/5/2009

HealthMedNet

Christmas Party 1945

Herman Eilts, a friend, Martha (my sister), John Becker, a friend, Elsie (my sister), me, Hilda (my sister)

Pentagon Plane Crash (1)

Pentagon Plane Crash (2)

Pentagon

A Personal Note

After working 30 years at the Pentagon and 20 years in private industry, I asked myself why I was still working. I decided then that I would really retire and commune with Mozart, play golf, ski, travel, read, write and develop a Web Page.

My wife and I decided to travel more and enjoy life. We visited our kids and grandchildren, traveled the United States, Europe, and took 60 cruises to the Caribbean, Canada, Bermuda, the Baltic capitols, Russia, the Mediterranean, Egypt, Israel, Turkey, Greece, England, Southeast Asia capitols, China and Hong Kong. In fact on one trip we traveled from Boston to Paris to Singapore to Hong Kong to San Francisco, to Boston - 33,000 miles around the world. We had a good life with our kids and grandchildren.

A few months before I started this book, my wife of 59 years died from cancer. Writing this book has been good therapy for my grief. She was a saint who spread God's love to everyone she met inspiring them to make their lives more loving and meaningful. I am deeply grateful for her love and for sharing her life with me for 59 years.

Contact author at

Res1@healthmednet.com